TERRY GILLIAM (Film Direc
'Twilight of the Gods' is an er
evening of ghosts, philosoph
brought to you via the torture
as he ends his days in a mac
spinning.'

Dr. TIMOTHY MADIGAN (Philosophy Now magazine)
Julian Doyle does a masterful job of using the two men's original material in an entertaining way. Expertly and cleverly playing on the theme of Wagner's 'Flying Dutchman', Doyle has the ghost of Wagner trapped in Nietzsche's cell until Nietzsche can redeem him.

BRUCE DICKINSON (Iron Maiden singer) *'Brilliant! I want all my friends to see it.'*

Prof. L. BRENT (Jewish Holocaust survivor)
'it was brilliantly conceived and acted, moving from serious argument to comedy and on to personal tragedy and confronting Wagner's anti-Semitism full on. As intelligent as it is entertaining'

TERRY JONES (Comedian/Historian)
'As intelligent and informative as any fun play could possibly get.'

PIPPA TENNANT (Edinburgh Festival Guide)
'How anyone could write such an intelligent, seem-less script analyzing the complex ideas of the composer Richard Wagner and the philosopher Friedrich Nietzsche is beyond me. Drawing much of his dialogue from the writings of the two stars, Julian Doyle succeeds magnificently.'

Chippenham Books 2ⁿᵈ EDITION

ISBN: 9781093817362

NIETZSCHE contra WAGNER

TWILIGHT

OF THE GODS

A play by

JULIAN DOYLE

'Wagner's opera is the
opera of redemption.
But who will redeem him.'

'The Wagner Case' *F. Nietzsche*

Some who cannot loosen their
own chains, can nonetheless
redeem their friends.'

'Thus Spake Zarathustra' *F. Nietzsche*

THE TURIN LUNATIC ASYLUM

11th January 1889

THE OVERTURE

On stage the last smudge of twilight comes through the
window. Nietzsche is 45 years old, he is thin and pale and
asleep in a chair, which he is strapped to. Papers are flung
around the floor. The lights fade as the Overture from
Wagner's 'Parsival' eases in gently. The door is unlocked
and a nursing sister comes in and picks up the papers.
Nietzsche stirs.

> NIETZSCHE
>
> Cosima?

The Nurse says nothing.

> NIETZSCHE
>
> Cosima?

> MATRON
>
> It's Matron, Signor Nietzsche, I'll just
> turn up the light.

She turns up the oil lamp as the music swells. Nietzsche
wakes. She checks his face and then undoes the straps on
his wrists.

> NIETZSCHE
>
> Am I alive?

MATRON
You are looking much better and very
much alive.

NIETZSCHE livens up.

NIETZSCHE
You think so but I need only talk with the
cultured people who come to Basel in
the summer to convince myself that I am
not alive. I am neither heard nor seen
nor....

MATRON
Don't excite yourself the headaches will
return. Here are your glasses I fixed
them and your papers are on the table.

She gives him the glasses, he sniffs the air.

NIETZSCHE
Where are the rabble I cannot smell
them?

MATRON
You are upstairs in a private room.

NIETZSCHE (exaggerated)
Did I free myself? Did my disgust itself
create wings and fly me to a height
where the rabble no longer sits at the
well.

MATRON
No, your mother sent money.

NIETZSCHE
Then do I have to listen to his music?

MATRON
What music?

NIETZSCHE
Ah. That's the reason I am imprisoned in this place.

MATRON
You are not imprisoned. Your mother and sister are on their way to take you home to Germany.

NIETZSCHE
Home! Turin is my home. Paris is my home, even the heights of Switzerland. The low lands are my hell. I can do anything - but to think German, to feel German, that is beyond my powers. I cannot even eat German: meat cooked to shreds, greasy and floury vegetables; the degeneration of puddings to paperweights.

MATRON
Feeling hungry are we? That's a good sign. I'll bring in your supper.

She leaves, locking the door behind her.

                    NIETZSCHE
          So she goes as do my disciples. Go away
          I tell them. Be alone. One repays a
          teacher badly if one remains only a pupil.
          Lose me and find yourselves. And then
          why should you not pluck at my laurels?
          (pause as if he hears an answer) What's
          that? You respect me, but how if one day
          your respect should tumble. Take care
          the falling statue does not strike you, as
          it struck me down.

                    GHOST
          Verwunder had mich, der mich erweckt.

(Translation: 'He who has awoken me has entranced me)

                    NIETZSCHE
          What's that rotting stench of decadence?

CARD –   1st MOVEMENT THE APPEARANCE

The music swells; Nietzsche adjusts his glasses. A dim
light magically reveals Wagner's Ghost in the corner.

                    NIETZSCHE
          What evokes this repugnant spectre to
          my scarred retina?

GHOST
Can I not visit an old friend and discuss
our eternal differences?

The voice is calm and humble in comparison.

NIETZSCHE
They told me you were dead. No, you
must be an illusion - a figment of my
imagination.

GHOST
Not at all, it is you who are a figment of
my imagination?

NIETZSCHE
Oh no. You're not going to be in charge of
my fantasy. For once you will be my
equal.

GHOST
Only in your fantasy could you be equal
to me.

NIETZSCHE
So that's the challenge that you come to
haunt me with is it?

GHOST
What can I say, Friedrich? My music
speaks for itself.

NIETZSCHE
Oh no, Maestro, your music speaks for
Schopenhauer. Your Mastersinger has to
stop and learn his philosophy before he
sings a note

GHOST
Why should he not sing philosophy,
would you rather he sang asinine
Kinderlied?

NIETZCHE
I would rather he sang revolution than
Schopenhaeurean capitulation.

GHOST
Must you thrash so wildly? He was once
your mentor, Herr Professor.

NIETZSHCE
Yes, in my blind days.

GHOST
Come on, Friedrich they were good days.
The three of us together like musketeers.

NIETZSCHE
You standing on your head and me and
Cosima laughing.

GHOST (laughs)
I did a lot of that didn't I?

NIETZSCHE
Every time you had a good idea – up you would go and stand on your head.

GHOST
Or climb a tree.

NIETZSCHER
Or climb a tree, or slide down the banisters. You convinced me that we don't stop playing because we grow old. We grow old because we stop playing.

GHOST
And we played a lot at putting the world to right with our philosophies didn't we?

NIETZSCHE
Do you remember the day I called on you and you were burning with passion for Hegel's 'Phenomenology'?

GHOST
Didn't I pronounce it - the best book ever written and to prove it I read you a passage.

NIETZSCHE
And since I didn't entirely follow it I asked you to read it again upon which neither of us could understand it.

GHOST
So I read it a third and fourth time until...

NIETZSCHE
In the end we both looked at each other
and burst out laughing.

GHOST
And that was the end of Hegel's
'Phenomenology.

They laugh heartily together.

A light brings in COSIMA laughing too.

COSIMA
Now what are you two laughing at?

GHOST
Hegel.

COSIMA
Hegel? Come, put on your boots and
Herr Professor you take my arm while
we walk and tell me what is so funny
about Hegel.

She puts out her arm and walks off as if together, and the
lights fade again. They fall into silent contemplation as
they remember.

NIETZSCHE
How is Cosima?

GHOST

She is fine. We sat together many nights re-reading Schopenhauer to the very end.

NIETZSCHE

You never laughed at Schopenhauer.

GHOST

No, but then his style was clear and precise. And yours Herr. Professor?

NIETZSCHE (proudly)

My style? It crunches up and destroys intellectual garbage on a heroic scale.

GHOST (aside)

If anyone could understand it.

NIETZSCHE

Doctor Heinrich von Stein once honestly complained that he understood not one word of my Zarathustra, I told him that was quite in order, to have understood six sentences of that book would have raised one to the highest level of mortals.

GHOST

To the Uebermensch; the Superman.

NIETZSCHE (smiles)
I often dream of you reading my books.

WAGNER magically pulls out a book.

GHOST
I have read your Autobiography.

NIETZSCHE
Ecce Homo. Behold the man.

GHOST
Pilot's words when the flagellated Christ
was brought before the rabble. Do you
come to redeem us as a Messiah?

NIETZSCHE
If I were a God I would hardly descend to
earth to waste time doing good acts and
then nihilistically dying to redeem man's
sins. Only a madman could come up with
such a ludicrous idea. No, I would come
down and do horrendous and sinful acts
and in that way take on myself man's
guilt, a much more useful and less self-
centred act.

GHOST
Are these the ideas you claim to be
ahead of their time?

NIETZSCHE
Far ahead, for some unfortunately are
born posthumously.

GHOST
Born posthumously? Are you mad?

NIETZSCHE
Yes, brilliantly and ferociously mad, for
in a mad world only the mad are sane

The GHOST opens the book.

GHOST
Sane! Look at the chapter headings in
your book? 'Why I am so Wise'. Chapter
two, 'Why I am so clever'. Chapter three,
'Why I write such Good Books'. That
could well be construed, at least, as a
lack of sane judgement.

NITZSCHE
Come Maestro, humility in an artist is as
false as truth is to a Politician. And you
for one have never doubted your operas
were the greatest the world has ever
known. You were just not brave enough
to say so. Although it slipped out on
many occasions like that interminable
speech you gave on the day we laid the
foundation stone for your Opera house
at Bayreuth?

GHOST (smiles)
Yes, Cosima kicked me under the table.

NIETZSCHE
Twice. She told me.

GHOST
Ahh, what a day that was.

NIETZSCHE (nostalgically)
What plans for the future.

GHOST
You see you were there at the birth of
my Opera House; you were Godfather to
my first child, you were one of the
family. Then suddenly you retreat and
produce these futile books.

NIETZSCHE
My reputation grows with every futile
failure. And you should know better than
any that it takes twenty years to become
an overnight success.

GHOST
But every failure brought you close to
suicide.

NIETZSCHE
It is always consoling to think on suicide:
in that way one gets through many a bad
night.

GHOST
But had you stayed I'm sure you would
have had success.

NIETZSCHE
Stay! After your despicable betrayal?

GHOST
I am totally ignorant of any harm I did
you.

NIETZSCHE (suddenly furious)
Liar, and I would ring out the truth out of
you, if I could get my hands on your
ghostly throat.

GHOST
Yes, they warned me that you were out
to kill me?

NIETZSCHE
And I would have - had you not died
before I could commit the deed.

Keys turn in the door and the MATRON enters with a tray.

MATRON
Supper.

NIETZSCHE (calm)
You see, I am visited by the celebrated
composer, Maestro Richard Wagner.

Nietzsche indicates the GHOST but
MATRON ignores the gesture.

                    MATRON
That's nice.

She places the tray across the arms of the chair.

                    GHOST
Who are you talking to?

                    NIETZSCHE
The nurse.

                    GHOST
You know perfectly well she's just a
figment of your imagination.

                    NIETZSCHE
That's rubbish.

                    MATRON
That's good wholesome food.

                    NIETZSCHE
Not the food. Its Wagner, he says you are
a figment of my imagination.

                    MATRON
You know in your deliriums you called
his name.

NIETZSCHE
Whose?

MATRON
Signor Wagner's, you called him father.

GHOST
I was a father to you.

NIETZSCHE
No, we were equals, that's what you
could never understand.

MATRON
No I understood it; you called him father
and asked for his forgiveness.

GHOST
So that is what brought you to this
fateful place. All the pretence of
knockabout attacks when really those
two books hurt you more than they hurt
me.

NIETZSCHE
I do not attack you personally.

MATRON
I should hope not.

NIETZSCHE
It quite clearly states in that book,

(indicates book, Matron looks round but sees nothing)

I only attack causes that are victorious. I employ the person as a strong magnifying glass to make visible a fallacy.

MATRON

I see.

GHOST

And what did your magnifying glass see in Wagner that was worthy of attack?

NIETZSCHE

I attacked Wagner for falseness and hybrid instincts, confusing the artful with the rich, and the late with the great.

MATRON

No, you shouted that you attacked Wagner because he betrayed you.

NIETZSCHE

Not at all. *(points at book, again Matron looks round)* It clearly states, I only attack people where any kind of personal difference is excluded. To be attacked by me is a proof of good will, even gratitude.

MATRON
Well you can keep that type of gratitude
to yourself.

She leaves sourly.

CARD – 2nd MOVEMENT. THE HISTORY.

A moment's silence as Nietzsche eats

GHOST
I never liked the society in which I found
myself. I stood shoulder to shoulder
with Bakunin at the Dresden uprising in
'49. I was banned from Germany for
twenty years for my revolutionary
activity. I starved in Paris, I begged from
the rich, I wrote music in cellars in Basel
hiding from my creditors till I was well
into my fifties.

NIETZSCHE
Whereas I at the age of 24, walk straight
out of College and into a Professorship at
Basel University where I meet the now
established Composer and Philosopher
who takes me aboard his star. I am not
blind to your point; you have earned the
right to be decadent whereas I have
earned the right to be grateful.

GHOST
No, I do not make that point at all. I just
don't see why a man at the barricades
should be attacked for societies faults.

NIETZSCHE finally rises slowly from his chair.

NIETZSCHE
But at the barricades you were an
optimist. You believed that this odious
society could be transformed -
Transformed by a theatre, an anarchist
theatre that would explode society and
usher in a new world.

GHOST
And I tried.

NIETZSCHE
You wanted every word to be clear,
every word a bombshell to be thrown at
private property.

GHOST
I hated Opera where the words were
banal and repetitive. Some lost in music
some even drowned out by other
singers.

NIETZSCHE
And right from my first visit you
expressed your love of Greek Drama and
the stature it held in their society.

Athenians didn't pay to see
performances. You assailed the
commercialisation of art, which turned,
what had been an end in itself into a
commodity.

GHOST
If I could stage an opera free I would but
it's impossible. Things change; even
philosophies are not set in stone.

NIETZSCHE
No, we can slip them around our social
conditions.

GHOST
I did not slip, I jumped, or more to the
point, I was thrown over the edge by
Schopenhauer.

NIETZSCHE (critically)
And why were you so irresistibly
attracted to him?

GHOST
Because one has to face truth.

NIETZSCHE
Or were you corrupted by the style
coruscating with ironic wit and
unforgettable metaphor?

GHOST

When I read Schopenhauer's *'World as Will and Representation'* I was an optimist, fighting for the political solutions that would transform society. But I was forced by Schopenhauer to make that difficult volte-face, and from this act of humiliation emerge anew.

NIETZCHE (disparagingly)

Humiliation?

GHOST

Humiliation, yes. Let me give an example, of which there are many. I was in London in 1855 at a friend's house for dinner. There was present a lady called Sissy Von Meysenbug, who had previously written a letter expressing enthusiastic agreement with my book *'The Work of Art of the Future'.* Over dinner I found her full of all kinds of plans to reform humanity similar to those I had set forth in my book, but which by then, under the influence of Schopenhauer I had abandoned. It was painful for me not to be understood by my enthusiastic friend and to be regarded by her as a renegade from a noble cause. We parted on very bad terms. I was accused by many of abandoning the revolution.

NIETZSCHE (firmly)
Let me tell you about your *'road to
Damascus'* conversion to Schopenhauer.

GHOST
It was not a conversion it was an act of
the intellect. I struggled to combat it but
the arguments were overpowering.

NIETZSCHE begins to get dangerously excited.

NIETZSCHE
Not at all, it was a conversion, because
like all of the converted you had reached
a stage in your life where you needed
Schopenhauer. More so you were
desperate for Schopenhauer, you craved
for Schopenhauer. He was your saviour,
your Messiah.

GHOST
You're raving mad.

Now NIETZSCHE becomes quiet and cunning.

NIETZSCHE
Am I? Have you already forgotten the
date of your disillusionment?

GHOST
My disillusionment?

NIETZSCHE
December 1851. Why for six months
after you even began every letter you
sent with that same date as if it was the
end of days.

GHOST
Oh yes. It was to me like a blow from hell
itself.

NIETZSCHE (disparagingly)
Why such pain?

GHOST
Think how close we were to the free
society we dreamed of. In 1848 the
French threw out King Louis and
brought in the second Republic. The
Young Italians were well on their way to
a united republic as were we the Young
Germans. The youthful America had
declared a Republic and those island
monkeys had a mad Hanoverian family
on a powerless throne. Then in May
1848 the Dresden uprising failed and I
was exiled. Then in 1851, the final straw;
the coup d'etat that brought that
imbecile Napoleon the third back to the
throne of France.

NIETZSCHE
Were you so naive that you could not
envisage a counter-revolution by the
forces of decadence? I could understand
your shock if, for instance, the Americans
had by their own free will, elected a
decadent imbecile president.

GHOST
Don't be preposterous.

CARD   3rd MOVEMENT. THE PHILOSOPHIES.

NIETZSCHE
So why then did you not advance from
Hegelian philosophy on to Feuerbach
and on to Marxism the natural
philosophical progression for a
revolutionary?

GHOST
Come on Herr. Professor, I was an
Anarchist.

NIETSZCHE
I grant you that the Anarchists and the
Marxists were strained bedfellows on
the barricades, but your retreat from the
fight virtually admits that Marx was right
about Utopian socialists. How did he
describe them? Ideologically self
indulgent to the point of soppiness and

worse than useless because the wishy-washy emotional guff moralising about love seduced the young who were well meaning but not hard thinking, making them ineffective. Does that not describe the Young Wagner?

GHOST

Certainly not, I could not follow that communist Rabbi or any philosophy that seemed to suggest that things were about to get better; I realized that tyranny and the abuse of power were perennial, as were cruelty, selfishness, greed, stupidity, and the failure of compassion. These were not merely a part of the current order of things, about to be swept away, they were permanent features of life on this planet, and were reproduced over and over again in every age.

The Ghost slips into depression, COSIMA enters and takes his hand.

NIETZSCHE

And so because you had advocated so forcefully that the role of art was to change society, this sudden disillusionment caused a despair, a paralysing despair, that Cosima told me, was almost clinical Now because there was no hope for the future of social change, there was no hope for the future of art, and therefore no hope for the future of Richard Wagner.

COSIMA
But Schopenhauer saved him?

NIETZSCHE
Saved him from what he called Jewish optimism. Our marooned musicologist had been blown off course and crashed his ship into the rocks of despair. He is shipwrecked, depressed and disorientated by the loss of an almost religious faith in political solutions. Then along comes the good ship Schopenhauer. Our marooned musicologist jumps aboard but instead of sailing off into open waters, our audacious captain Schopenhauer cleverly steers his ship with energetic purpose directly at the same rocks crashing it to pieces. Why? Because he has a new way of looking at the world, a way that declares that being shipwrecked is the purpose of life, a view that saw politics, as trivial, and positively advocating disillusionment - marooning oneself from the world and its contrived values. Moreover our audacious Captain declares that the only valuable human activity is sexual love

and the arts and selecting above all others the art of music as the most important. What was your favourite saying?

COSIMA
How can I thank him enough?

She pats the ghosts hand and leaves.

NIETZSCHE
How can he thank him enough indeed for the philosophy he required, worked out on a scale and at a level of genius that could not be ignored and advocating none other than the very art of music as its centre-point. Now the possibility of a retreat to the Buddhist temple with not a stitch of guilt, well perhaps a smidgen of discomfort as you face Mrs Von Meysenbug and the others whom you soon learn to dismiss as uninitiated.

The GHOST is silent. NIETZSCHE sits back down.

GHOST (thoughtfully)
My so called need for Schopenhauer does not invalidate his ideas. Lasting happiness and fulfilment can never be found in a world in which frustration, suffering and death are the inevitable lot of everyone; to seek to attain happiness and fulfilment by any worldly activity is -

to be deluded. It is not just that the conditions on which we happen to have been offered life in this world are unacceptable - any life in this world is undesirable.

NIETZSCHE is about to reply but the GHOST continues with mounting enthusiasm as he warms to his task as the music swells with his enthusiasm.

GHOST
In fact we do not belong on this planet at all; our existence here is fleeting and illusionary, and what is permanent about us is outside space and time. This means that the function of art is not, and could not possibly be, to unveil some future state or point the way towards it. The true role of art is something radically different. At the most superficial level it is an escape from the intolerable world into an alternative one. The true values of art are such as to be centred outside the empirical world altogether, outside the realm of space and time – art speaks of ultimate and permanent values, of ultimate and permanent existence. Willing, wanting, longing, craving, yearning, these are not just things that we do, they are what we are and when music speaks it is entirely out of our power not to feel these expectations and desires. These responses have nothing to

do with our knowledge. We feel the music, it stirs emotions, the patterns of chords can leave us suspended waiting for the resolution in the tonic. Music like life is the perpetual creation and spinning out of longing, stretching us out as on a rack, unable ever to accept where we are as a resting place, until the complete cessation of everything – the end of the piece or the end of the individuals life. Music can make us love or it can make us go to war. It can move us to tears and raise us to..

NIETZSCHE (shouts)
RAISE US TO SILENCE I wish! Will not my own apparition allow me a word in edgeways? This facsimile is certainly as verbose as the original.

GHOST
I have to make clear the philosophy.

NIETZSCHE
But you don't have to give me the full canon – I have after all read it myself.

GHOST
And *you* were stricken by the genius of his labour too.

NIETZSCHE
For different reasons.

GHOST
Which were?

NIETZSCHE
I was young and although I felt equal to you in discussing my subject, Greek drama, I could hardly match you in other subjects. Especially one so fanatically and robustly advocated.

GHOST
I see I bullied you into Schopenhauer.

NIETZSCHE
No I had been seduced before I met you, but you did brow beat everyone you met about philosophy and music, especially your friends.

GHOST
Natural enthusiasm.

NIETZSCHE
The truth is - I stayed with Schopenhauer because of my most disastrous of character traits.

GHOST
What foolishness, you were the nicest
and pleasantest young man. There were
no disastrous character traits.

NIETZSCHE
Yes there were - I desperately wanted to
please people.

GHOST
Is that a fault?

NIETZSCHE
When it prevents critical analysis. You
hardly noticed that towards the end I
was feeling stressed as I developed ideas
which were un-Schopenhaurian. I began
drifting away, trying to find space to
think - to express my *self*.

GHOST
That caused you to abscond and desert
our friendship?

NIETZSCHE
No. That was something else. I have
work to do.

NIETZSCHE sits down at the desk and
picks up his pen and tries to think.

GHOST
What was it? You have never explained
yourself.

NIETZSCHE
I'm not prepared to talk about it.

WAGER
Why ever not?

NIETZSCHE
Never you mind.

GHOST
I think that's the height of rudeness to
attack and not explain why.

NIETZSCHE
You forget, I am the premiere champion
of rudeness. Rudeness must not be
undervalued it is the highest form of
human form of contradiction.

GHOST
Is that what created this iconoclastic
style of writing.

NIETZSCHE
My epic battle against the twin evils of
good manners and good naturedness
produces ferocious words thrown like
thunderbolts.

GHOST
Or perhaps, if you will forgive me, it was just a response to your loneliness, isolation and lack of success?

NIETZSCHE (saddened)
You're right, I was lonely, lonelier than any man could imagine. I was desolate, isolated, humiliated and unheard day in day out.

GHOST
I'm sorry but it was you who walked away from us.

NIETZSCHE
Why be sorry? Have you not read my epistle to my disciples? 'I wish on them suffering, sickness, being forsaken – mistrust of oneself and the torture of self contempt.' For only blood soaked words can grasp truth.

GHOST
Did you bleed a lot when you wrote those two books against me?

NIETZSCHE
Tragically I am the only one who could understand the harm that Schopenhauer did to your libretto.

GHOST
What harm?

NIETZSCHE
Look at your operas.

CARD - 4th MOVEMENT. THE OPERAS

GHOST
Not the first three I beg of you. They
were just copies of French and Italian
spectaculars. I have banned them all
from the Opera House at Bayreuth even
after my death.

NIETZSCHE
I can ignore your French and Italian
Operas if you wish, as you soon realized
they were decadent forms - with no
future. But the 'Fairies' is a brilliant and
precocious work for a twenty year old.

GHOST
Yes it is good isn't it. And it did show me
there was still a lot to be done with the
Supernatural sagas of German
romanticism.

NIETZSCHE
Which you did with, 'Tannhauser',
'Lohengrin' and 'The Flying Dutchman'
each one a masterpiece.

GHOST
And you expect me to carry on a form I
had exhausted of all developmental
possibilities?

NIETZSCHE
I agree, poltergeist, there was nowhere
else to go with German Romanticism, so
you stopped while you theorized about
the future producing your definitive
books, 'Opera and Drama' and 'The work
of Art of the Future'. Oh and also
producing three illegitimate children
with your conductor's wife.

The GHOST shrugs apologetically.

GHOST
Stick to the point.

NITZSCHE
Then after five years you set yourself the
task of composing opera in your new
theoretical form, the four operas of the
Ring.

GHOST
No. I started by writing 'Siegfried' but for
some reason, people found the story too
complicated so I was forced to write
'Rhinegold', Valkerie' and
'Gotterdammerung'.

NITZSCHE (sarcastically)
Complicated? What's so complicated,
Siegfried is the son of his uncle and the
nephew of his mother. He is his own
cousin. He is also the nephew of his wife
and son of his aunt and therefore his
own uncle by marriage. He is the son-in-
law of his grandfather Wotan, the
brother-in-law of his aunt, who is at the
same time his mother. And of course
Siegmund is the father-in-law to his
sister Brunnhilde and the brother-in-law
of his son, and that's not all..

GHOST
That's enough.

NIETZSCHE (laughs)
Chaos reigns in the Ring Family and
incest is rife.

GHOST
Incest was a symbol of innocence versus
the civilized.

NIETZSCHE
Perhaps, but after the first two Operas
the disillusionment and despair set in. A
paralysis for twelve long years.

GHOST
Till Schopenhauer saved me so how can
you criticize him?

NIETZSCHE
I don't, at this point, criticise him. I
criticise you - because what *was* this
despair that paralysed you?

GHOST
But you've already told us Political
disillusionment. Have you become
boringly repetitive in your madness?

NIETZSCHE
Not at all I think with such crystal clarity
that my neighbours are in danger of
catching a severe cold and if you
wouldn't mind, spirit, kindly refrain from
insulting your creator.

The GHOST raises a hand apologetically.

NIETZSCHE
Your disillusionment did not come for
the reasons you gave and I would have
told you if you hadn't bolted with such
an interminably long speech that I forgot
where the hell I was by the time I
managed to rein you in.

GHOST
If I am not to insult you then I ask Herr
Professor, that the same courtesy should
be shown to the deceased.

The two nod to each other in acceptance.

GHOST
So what reason do you give for my grand
imperfection?

NIETZSCHE
Firstly, King Ludwig the Second.

GHOST
King Ludwig was my benefactor.

NIETZSCHE
And Cosima.

GHOST
Cosima! My wife? You *have* completely
lost your reason.

NIETZSCHE (overblown)
Think on this, here is our disillusioned
republican failing to explode the status
quo, exiled from Germany and hounded
from every other country by creditors
when suddenly from across the rainbow
approaches an angelic eighteen year old
King with the proverbial pot of gold.

GHOST (smile of
remembrance)
When his representatives first appeared
asking questions I took them for
creditors and turned tail and ran?

NIETZSCHE
I know it took them three long months to
finally catch up with you - and bring all
hope of anarchist, republican furore to
an end.

GHOST
King Ludwig relieved me of perpetual
financial worries.

NIETZSCHE
His royal gold relieved you of any critical
analysis of society.

GHOST
And Cosima?

NIETZSCHE
She made you happy.

GHOST
Happy?

The Ghost dismisses this and sits down.

CARD – 5th MOVEMENT. THE LITTLE WOMAN.

NIETZSCHE
Our debauched fifty year old anarchist
suddenly meets an attractive girl half his
age, who happens to be the illegitimate
daughter of Franz Liszt. So not only is
she intelligent but she understands
music. And against all his principals he
marries her and with his royal gold
settles into a bourgeois existence.

GHOST
Against my principles?

NIETZSCHE
Does not Sieglinde sing, 'This house and
this woman are owned by Hunding' -
expressing your original objection that
marriage makes the woman an object of
ownership – a domestic animal,
something to be loved down to.

GHOST
Cosima and I were equals, not in any
shape or form the way you refer to the
opposite sex as 'the little woman', a
dangerous, creeping, subterranean little
beast of prey.

NIETZSCHE

Ahh, but so pleasant with it. That's the reason to beware of emancipation since the little woman is unspeakably more wicked than the man, also cleverer. Goodness in a woman is already a form of degeneration.

GHOST

And love?

NIETZSCHE

Love is, in its methods – war, in its foundations the mortal hatred of the sexes. The only way to cure a woman - to redeem her, is to make a child for her. The woman has need of children, the man is only the means.

GHOST

I cannot tell whether this is comedy, bitterness or revenge for the curse inflicted on you.

NIETZSCHE

All base human emotions, but we were talking about your hypocrisy. In your Operas you value the honest spontaneous feelings of the human heart. These values are seen as shocking and unacceptable by society - as was your relationship with Cosima. On the other side are the values embodied by such basic institutions as property and marriage, which are taken for granted by society as elementary to civilization, but was seen as shocking and unacceptable by you. The collision between the two in your operas is always cataclysmic; and those who live by the heart must expect to be crushed by society. Your heroic destruction of Siegfried and Brunnhilde, in the Ring and of Tristram and Isolde, express these deep held beliefs. So then why on earth did you betray these principles and marry.

The GHOST looks down repentantly.

> GHOST
> Well.. because Cosima wanted it.

> NIETZSCHE (delighted)
> Ah ha! The little woman wins again. A comedy of pathos.

The door opens and in comes the MATRON.

> MATRON
> Finished have we?

> NIETZSCHE
> Speak of the Devil.

She begins to clear the tray.

                    GHOST
Women are not devils; sexual
intercourse is the highest of all human
activities provided it is an act of love
embraced freely on both sides.

                    NIETZSCHE
Provided après sex they give their lives
to you in the final sacrifice.

                    MATRON (Alarmed)
You're not going to remove your clothes
and dance around again, are you?

                    NIETZSCHE
That representation was of the orgiastic
frenzy that lies at the root of Greek
tragedy.

                    MATRON (suspiciously)
Was it?

                    NIETZSCHE
Dance is joyous levity, the antithesis of
gravity.

                    GHOST
I agree.

NIETZSCH
In the Flying Dutchman – the woman
sacrifices herself to release our ancient
mariner from the curse of existence.

MATRON
I know the opera well.

GHOST
Redemption is the highest form of Love.

NIETZSCHE
And how does one explain the end of
Tristram and Isolde?

MATRON (earnestly)
Isolde dies of a broken heart.

NIETZSCHE
She sits there over the dead body of
Tristram and just swoons to death.

MATRON
It's a measure of her love.

NIETZSCHE
It's ridiculous. Wagner's heroines are
much given to dying from no apparent
cause.

MATRON
It's beautiful.

GHOST
There you see.

MATRON
You have no sense of romance.

NIETZSCHE
Romance? I am in love with everything.

MATRON
Its chilly I will open up the fire.

GHOST
Sehnen *(translation = Longing)*. Longing is
the essence of Tristram and Isolde.
Longing for each other, longing for the
night when they can meet, longing for
death.

NIETZSCHE
Longing for Schopenhauer. What is it
they sing? 'Let us die and never part –
united – nameless – endless – no more
Tristram – no more Isolde'.

MATRON
That's my favourite part.

MATRON leaves humming to the music.

GHOST
There is no trick in her feelings.

NIETZSCHE

Of course there is. The little woman
does not read the Philosophy of love. She
feels it as a basic instinct. Really she
knows death that brings all to an end is
not a measure of love. She hangs on to
life like a gecko. It is the stupid man who
falls for this guff about love. Women fain
suicide as a tactic, men actually do it.
How many times did your jealous love
demand from Cosima that final sacrifice
after your death? Don't deny it.

GHOST (guiltily)

Well... yes, we did agree such a pact.

NIETZSHE (enjoying this)

Of course she agreed. But then after
death you waited - one day, two days, a
week and then, oh the disappointment it
must have been. Waiting in nothingness
for Cosima to join you. But she's no
senseless romantic; she knows,
nothingness is nothingness and is of
little interest to the life giving 'Little
Woman'.

GHOST

It was important for her to carry on my
work at Bayreuth, to bring together all
my writings at the library. So much to do.

NIETZSCHE
Is that how you accommodate your
disappointment. No, the truth is she saw
your Schopenhauer philosophy for what
it is - an egocentric escape to the Tibetan
heights of a Buddhist temple.

GHOST
No, it is a philosophy that teaches one to
disentangle oneself from the day to day
and look on the bigger picture.

NIETSCHE
Or an excuse by the middle aged as to
why they can dismiss their youthful
selves.

CARD -   6th MOVEMENT. THE MIDDLE AGED.

GHOST
There is a wisdom in the middle age.

NIETZSCHE
There is also a defector. See how the
Ring Cycle is kidnapped by the middle
aged. You begin with 'Siegfried' a young
anarchist who asserts that the exercise
of political power is incompatible with
the natural order of things. Nature is
idyllic and the imposition of government
is an unnecessary evil. But to build
Valhalla, the middle aged Wotan civilizes

by the use of his spear of destiny, the symbol of State power. Then because the story is too complex you write pre-stories, 'The Rhinegold' and 'Valkyrie' But during this process you are seduced by Schopenhauer. And in the new explanatory operas Wotan dethrones our young Anarchist Siegfried from the starring role. He becomes the baritone voice of reason singing two operas before Siegfried even makes an appearance. Fortuitously the anarchist ending still remains where our young Siegfried sweeps aside Wotan and with his own death brings the whole existing order crashing down.

GHOST

That can be construed as a Schopenhauer ending.

NIETZSCHE

Anarchist or Schopenhauerian is not the point. What you see here is the seeds of a traitors ending.

GHOST

How so?

NIETZSCHER

Because in your next Opera, 'The Mastersingers of Nuremburg' the seed has germinated into an over ripe putrid fruit. Here again the lead tenor has little respect for existing authority and is impatient to sweep it aside. When along comes the middle aged bass baritone, Hans Sachs who..

He indicates for the ghost to take over.

> GHOST
> Explains to the young man that the existing order is a repository of accumulated wisdom from the past, so that while it is important to root out the dead and decaying, it is also essential to recognise the good and carry that forward into the future.

> NIETZSCHE (Viciously)
> The middle age are traitors who call it virtuous when their vices grow lazy.

> GHOST
> Not at all, the older man has a deeply compassionate understanding of the way things are. Youth is a wonderful thing but it is a dreadful shame that it is wasted on the young.

> NIETZSCHE
> So what does one do when confronted by the enfant terrible who used to be oneself?

GHOST
One educates him to perceive and
appreciate what is good in the existing
order.

NIETZSCHE
Not only appreciate the existing order
but actually to take a leading position in
it. In Mastersingers our young genius
who once poured scorn on society, ends
up as its standard bearer and an
acclaimed leader of the establishment.

GHOST
It is life's tragedy, we get old too soon
and wise too late.

NIETZSCHE
Was it wisdom or feeble old age that sent
you fearful and trembling towards the
Christian cross. And writing the libretto
to that final abomination. Parsival?

NIETZSCHE grabs a crucifix from above the bed and
waves at the Ghost.

GHOST
Come now what fault can you find in this
mystic tale of the knights who guard the
Christian relics of the Holy Grail?

NIETZSCHE (disgusted)
To be worthy of this task a knight has to
be celibate? You, who in your youth
ravaged anything and everything in
sight, now in senility demand chastity. Is
this your Shopenhauerian escape from
earthly passions? Where poor Klingsor
who is too wholesome to control his
sexual lusts castrates himself to join the
knights. Is that what the old have to
teach the young?

GHOST (defensively)
No Klingsor's mutilation does not make
him worthy.

NIETZSCHE
Exactly. After he makes this dreadful
sacrifice he is still barred and so
becomes your evil one, surrounding
himself with a band of nymphettes who
do battle with the Knights seducing them
one by one till they are sapped of all
energy. This is typical Christian - anti-
life sentiment from one who in his youth
detested the ridiculous religious
superstitions.

GHOST
But I am prepared to talk about the all
important and fundamental truths

50

contained in Christianity or any other religion.

NIETZSCHE
The only fundamental truth is that God is a comedian playing to an audience too afraid to laugh.

He tosses the crucifix on the bed

CARD - 7th MOVEMENT. THE ANTICHRIST

The Matron comes in.

MATRON
It's bedtime.

She notices the crucifix on the bed, shakes her head and starts to replace it on the wall

GHOST
You have a closed mind.

NIETZSCHE
Do I have a closed mind, Sister?

MATRON
You have a confused mind, and please don't move our Lord.

NIETZSCHE (to the Ghost)
Can you prove there is a God?

MATRON
Of course. Who made the universe?

NIETZSCHE
I don't know. Who did?

MATRON
God did. And who put life on the earth.

NIETZSCHE
I don't know, who did?

MATRON
God did. And who made man?

NIETZSCHE
I don't know who did?

MATRON
God did. And there's your proof.

NIETZSCHE
Very good, and who moved the crucifix?

MATRON
You did.

NIETSZCHE
How do you know it wasn't God?

MATRON
Don't be silly. I'll be back in a minute to
turn off the light.

She leaves. NIETZSCHE points after her.

NIETZSCHE
That's the closed mind for you.
Explaining all the great mysteries of life
with one simple certainty – God. But in
fact when faced with a minor question
like who moved the crucifix – she knows
very well God didn't do it.

GHOST
You really are a dreadful cynic.

NIETZSCHE
The rare power of accurate observation
is commonly called cynicism by the
those who have not got it, and even
common sense is not so common.

GHOST
What is common is a belief in a God. It is
universal.

NIETZSCHE
So why did then with all these Gods did
our arch anti-Semite choose a Jewish
Messiah?

GHOST
He was not Jewish; it has been proved by
my English son in law, Houston
Chamberlain that Christ was of Arian

53

descent. And anyway I am not against using a good story from any source.

NIETZSCHE
A chaste story of suppressed sexuality. How could you; the very person who regarded the sexual act as the highest expression of love and hated Christianity that looked upon it as sinful, dirty and supercharged with hateful guilt? You even regarded Christianity as incompatible with art. What happened, did your aged mortality make a coward of you or is it your organs that have desiccated?

GHOST (with reverence)
I was moved by the sacred in face of the cruel state of the world.

NIETZSCHE
The only excuse God has for the cruel state of the World is that he doesn't exist. It is all superstitious babble.

GHOST
And how many of the Nietzsche family help spread this superstitious babble, since Luther nailed his thesis on the church door? Ten, Eleven, thirteen?

NIETZSCHE
Twenty Ministers.

GHOST
Twenty Ministers! Including your father.
And what did they call the young Fritz,
for his devotion to the word?

NIETZSCHE
The little Minister.

GHOST
In declaring yourself the antichrist and
trumpeting that God is dead you have
certainly put your neck on the block in
the hereafter.

NIETZSCHE
Not only is he dead but I take pride in
having killed him.

GHOST
I worry, in this state are you ready to
meet your maker?

NIETZSCHE
I'm ready to meet my maker but is he
ready to meet me, that's the question.

CARD - 8th MOVEMENT. THE EXORCISM

GHOST

So you do not believe in mysticism, or in the supernatural?

NIETZSCHE

No I don't.

The GHOST circles NIETZSCHE and whispers in his ear.

GHOST

So how do you explain me being here when I died four years ago?

NIETZSCHE

You are just a figment of my miraculous imagination capable of any twist and turn I wish to make on you.

GHOST

No, within your imagination I am still a disturbing entity, able to act freely in spite of you. You cannot exorcise me because I am a tormenting dream that will never be resolved by reason.

NIETSCHE (fiercely)

You forget I am the most terrible human being there has ever existed, my philosophies have unmasked Christian morality, an event without equal, a destiny, breaking world history into two parts. Those who have come before me and those who will follow.

GHOST

Take care you cannot exorcise a memory without an intrusive operation on the brain.

NIETZSCHE jumps from the chair and turns on the Ghost.

NIETZSCHE

Can't I? Watch me exorcise you with intellect. By the time I have finished with you - you will be on your knees begging to return to oblivion.

GHOST (sits down)

I see you have delusions of grandeur too?

NIETZSCHE

You, spirit, are the most selfish object that ever existed. And all your theorizing was merely justification. You are a prime example of Fichte's dictum that 'each of us has the philosophy he has because he is the person he is'. Only a Zarathustra can conceive of the reality outside of himself.

GHOST

A Superman, like you.

NIETZSCHE (vigorously)
A superman like me cannot fool himself
like you. Your Anarchism was not really
a political anarchism it was a belief that
you personally should be allowed to do
what the hell you liked and nobody
should stop you. Your advocacy against
morals was just a sham to allow you free
range with every husband's wife that
came under your spell. Even your
devotion to Schopenhauer came from
the shallowness of your politics. You lied
and cheated not only others but mainly
yourself. You borrowed immense
quantities of money and then justified
your absconding by announcing to the
world that you didn't believe in private
property. And then you attacked those
who loaned you money by attacking
their race.

CARD - 9th MOVEMENT. THE JEW

GHOST (defensively)
That is not true my argument against the
Jew was reasoned and purely theoretical.
I laid it out in my pamphlet, 'Jewishness
in Music'.

NITZSCHE (attacking)
It was pure racism, the only thing that
can be said in your favour is that you
never advocated discrimination. You just
vented your spleen against them.

GHOST (reasonably)
My hostility was cultural. The recent
emancipation of the Jew brought about
their release into the main body of
German society at a time when that
society had not had time to establish its
own identity and was therefore unable
to cope with so powerful an invasion of
alien influence.

NIETZSCHER
Oh, you were a little firmer than that.
You called it a corrupting influence on
German intellectual and artistic life that
had to be destroyed.

GHOST
The reason I hated them, just as I hated
the French, was I - like all
revolutionaries wanted a united
Germany, un-dominated and
uncontaminated by non-German cultural
influences. We hoped for national
regeneration as proud custodian of the
greatest of all traditions in the greatest
of all the arts, music. Why should we feel

inferior to the French, we had, Bach,
Beethoven, Liszt, Mendelssohn..

NITZSCHE
Mendelssohn was a Jew.

GHOST (angrily)
I have nothing against the Jew!

He recovers his composure.

it is just that they descended on us
Germans too soon, we were not yet
stable enough to absorb them.

NIETZSCHE
Don't backtrack, your pamphlet called
them an unpleasant freak of nature.
Furthermore you said, 'on stage we can
not conceive of a character, historical or
modern, hero or lover, being played by a
Jew without feeling the absurdity of such
an idea.'

GHOST
I revised that in the reprint of the
pamphlet in 1868.

NIETZSCHE
Yes. Because by that time there were
Jews playing romantic leads all over the

place, exposing the nonsense of the
original.

GHOST (smugly)
There, I am open to change.

NIETZSCHE
No you are not. You make no real
intellectual changes or decisions. They
are all made emotionally. Even your anti-
Semitism is pure emotion and I can
prove it.

GHOST
Prove what?

NIETZSCHE
That your anti-Semitism is all emotion

GHOST (laughs)
Go ahead, prove it then.

NIETZSCHE
When you went to Paris, to the centre of
Operatic culture you wrote the Opera
'Rienzi' that you have since described as
your secret shame.

GHOST
My family and myself were starving we
needed money.

61

NIETZSCHE
The style of that Opera was identical to
the most famous composer in Paris at
the time, who was..?

GHOST
Meyerbeer.

NIETZSCHE
Whose Operas you later described in
your writings as..?

GHOST
Manufactured nonsense. What are you
driving at?

NIETZSCHE goes to his desk and picks
up a letter.

NIETZSCHE
I'll tell you what I'm driving at – what I
am driving at is your real secret shame,
the letter.

GHOST (horrified)
No. How.. where did you..?

NIETZSCHE
Oh yes. Your library has received copies..

GHOST
No they couldn't have.

NIETZSCHE
Yes they could – it reveals the depths of
sycophantic, debasement and deception
to which you could stoop.

GHOST
No!

The GHOST reaches over for the letter but NIETZSCHE
pulls it away and reads.

NIETZSCHE (exaggeratedly)
You (Meyerbeer) are everything to me,
everything. I have reached the point of
having to sell myself, in order to obtain
help in the most material sense of the
word. But my head and my heart are no
longer mine to give away, they are your
property, my master, the most that is left
to me is my two hands. Do you wish to
make use of them? I realize that I must
become your slave..

GHOST
Stop this, I was desperate.

NIETZSCHE
Who is this Meyerbeer who has
witnessed your shame and total
humiliation? A Jew. One of the race in
Paris who you, in your paranoid way,
swore were conspiring to help one
another by doing down non Jews.

GHOST (angrily)
So they were. The two top composers in Paris were Meyerbeer and Halevey who were both Jews supported by Jewish music publishers and critics.

NIETZSCHE (calmly)
So who gave you money and arranged to put on your opera 'Rienzi'?

GHOST
Meyerbeer - but in Dresden not in Paris.

NIETZSCHE
And did this Jew not give you more money to get your 'Flying Dutchman' performed in Berlin? Yes. And after writing (reads again) 'I shall be a loyal and honest slave who one day will tell you of my gratitude.' What do you do? Within the year as you still did not think your career was advancing fast enough you began to hate those who had witnessed your humiliation. And under a pseudonym you write 'that Halevey was not a deliberately cunning swindler like Meyerbeer'. Grateful, not at all. Irrationally paranoid and vindictively spiteful. All your life you exploited Jews to advance your career, you borrowed huge quantities of money from them..

GHOST

There you see. They are all money-
grabbing moneylenders out to exploit
my poverty.

NIETZSCHE

Oh. You just said they were composers
and music publishers but what they
really are; are tailors. I mean where else
could you get a decent suit other than
from a Jew?

NIETZSCHE laughs.

GHOST

You can afford to laugh, but you have
never seen your family destitute the way
we starved in Paris.

NIETZSCHE

You could have got a job. No you, like all
artists, they will exploit everyone and
everything around them in the name of
their art.

The GHOST jumps up and heads for the
centre of the room, and raises his arms.

GHOST

I have had enough of this torment.

SHOUTS OUT

Return me to eternal sleep.

65

There is a clap of thunder and lightening but when the Ghost looks at himself, he is still there. NIETZSCHE laughs

NIETZSCHE
I am sorry, Herr Composer, like the Flying Dutchman you are now stuck here. Stuck in an existence from which you cannot escape, until you can redeem yourself. Or perhaps have someone sacrifice themselves for your redemption.

GHOST (calls off)
Cosima!

NIETZSCHE
No. She was a figment of my imagination not yours and I forbid her to appear

GHOST
Wait. You, yes you can redeem me. In spite of your sour comments you have made tonight, did you not write here in your biography that your days spent with Cosima and me were the happiest days of your life?

NIETCHE
Yes they were, and I could have
redeemed you if you had not cruelly
betrayed me.

GHOST
What this betrayal that caused you to
leave at the moment of my triumph?

NIETZSCHE
There are two betrayals. My leaving was
your betrayal of yourself. Your betrayal
of me happened later.

GHOST (exasperated)
For pity's sake explain yourself.

CARD   10th MOVEMENT. THE BETRAYAL

NIETZSCHE
As one of your inner circle I had lived
every moment of getting the Bayreuth
opera house built, embracing like a
religion your desire to revolutionize the
whole of contemporary art and society.
But then came the horrific night in 1876.

GHOST
The launch of the Opera House?

NIETZSCHE

Yes. Suddenly there before my eyes were the upper bourgeoisie of the new Kaiser-reich in full plumage, radiating chauvinist triumphalism after the victory over France.

GHOST

Why shouldn't they celebrate a victory against Napoleon the third? Why you participated in the war yourself as an orderly.

Ride of the Valkyries Music begins to creep in.

NIETZSCHE

Mistakenly, for it has now become clear to me that it is much better to lose a war rather than to win one.

GHOST

How so?

NIETZSCHE

Well if you lose then the despotic leaders who got you into the war in the first place, slump home to be over-thrown by a critical population, as was Napoleon the third. If you win then everyone struts home waving banners, banging drums and blowing their brains out through their trumpets - looking for the next fight with anyone to show off their new bogus superiority. And there they all were at Bayreuth, the whole idle Royal riff-raff swaggering around and glorifying the Holy German Spirit that your Opera had captured so perfectly. German Spirit, I'll tell you the origin of German spirit - disturbed intestines. Why these charming Herr Teutons have such a fearful appetite that they can nourish themselves on opposites gulping 'faith' as well as 'science', 'Christian Love' as well as 'Anti-Semitism', 'Will to power, to the Kaiser-reich, as well as the epistle to the humble. No wonder they have such a massive indigestion that produces canisters of bad air that my nose demands my retreat.

GHOST
So that's why you left?

NIETZSCHE (angrily)
The smell of decadence is everywhere, but I could have stomached it had I not had to watch Herr Composer, blissfully allowing himself to be wrapped in this Germanic cloak. And nauseatingly making up to every royal patron as if they were important; scarcely finding time to talk to the likes of Professor

69

Nietzsche or the others who had sweated for the cause. The cause was now auctioned off to the highest bidder and all that mattered to Richard Wagner was his recognition and remuneration.

GHOST
Was Professor Nietzsche hurt by my betrayal of the ideas or by my lack of attention to him?

NIETZSCHE (sadly)
I have become used to lack of attention, especially from Germans. Why the only place my philosophies are taught is in Copenhagen.

GHOST
So that's why you refused to come to the launch of 'Parsifal' unless I personally invited you as the most honoured guest? I'm sorry I received the letter too late.

NIETZSCHE
Luckily for there was Richard Wagner, apparently at his most triumphant, but in truth a decaying and despairing decadent, sank down, helpless and broken, before the Christian cross. Did no German have eyes in his head or pity in his conscience for this horrid spectacle?

WAGER
Was this my betrayal?

NIETZSCHE
Of yourself but exactly one year on, you
betrayed me.

GHOST
But we never met you in 1877.

NIETZSCH
No

GHOST
Tell me.

NIETZSCH
It was when I went to visit Doctor Eiser
in Frankfurt. He detected in me severe
and irreversible damage to the retinas of
my eyes and a chronic inflammation of
the central nervous system, which was
the cause of my severe headaches.

WAGER
Yes.

NIETZSCHE (hesitantly)
Dr. Eiser happened to be a devoted fan of
yours and had written an essay on your
Ring Cycle, which he asked me to hand
on to you.

GHOST

Yes, I remember it well, he wrote saying
your health was bad and enclosed his
essay. I promptly replied to him with a
full estimation of his work.

NIETZSCHE

Asking him in your letter what exactly
was wrong with me?

GHOST

That's right, although we hadn't spoken
for over a year I still cared for you. and
he replied very sympathetically that alas
there was a serious possibility of you
going blind.

NIETZSCHE (hurt)

You then carried on a correspondence
with him that was leaked to everyone in
Bayreuth including Cosima.

GHOST

No.

NIETZSCHE

You did, Lou Salome attended Bayreuth
Festival that year with my sister and sent
me the niceties of your reply.

He grabs the letter and reads.

'In assessing Nietzsche's condition I have long been reminded of identical experiences with young men of great ability. Seeing them laid low by similar symptoms, I have discovered all too certainly that these were the effects of masturbation.'

GHOST (apologetically)
I wanted to help.

NIETZSCHE
So Dr. Eiser writes back, 'I am bound to accept your assumption because I too am led by many aspects of Nietzsche's behaviour to regard it as all to credible. Given the well known tenacity of the vice, I would be dubious of any method of treatment.' To which you reply..

He hands the letter to the Ghost who reads it apprehensively.

GHOST
'Your patient spoke to me of gonorrhoeal infections during his student days and also that he recently had intercourse several times in Italy on medical advise.

NIETZSCHE puts his head down in his hands in despair.

GHOST (cont)
This demonstrates that our patient lacks the capacity for satisfying his sexual urge

in a normal manner; a circumstance which is conceivable in masturbators of his age..' – Please Friedrich, I didn't mean..

NIETZSCHE (dangerously)
How could you! The abysmal treachery! You are so rich in malicious ideas even to the extent of leaking an exchange of letters with my doctor to voice your opinion that my criticism of you was just a consequence of unnatural excess, with hints at pederasty.

GHOST
No, I never hinted at such a thing.

NIETZSCHE (distraught)
And presumably discussing the whole thing with Cosima. And then you ask me for redemption.

GHOST
You must believe me I never leaked that letter. All I can imagine is that Hans von Wolzogen the archivist at Bayreuth was the culprit. I would never.. and come to think of it, I'm afraid Dr. Eiser on purely ethical grounds should not have entered into that correspondence.

NIETZSCHE

No! There are no excuses. You are now
marooned here as cursed as the Flying
Dutchman because there is nothing that
can redeem you.

GHOST

I only wished the best of health for you.
Please believe me.

NIETZSCHE

Accept that you are in every way a
blaggard.

GHOST (sullenly)

You are right - right in every detail?
Every criticism, every slander, I am
totally worthless.

NIETZSCHE

No. That won't save you; we have
already seen the depths to which you
will humiliate yourself to get your way.

GHOST

This is a pain worse than death.

NIETZSCHE

Craving for the Shopenhauerian end to
existence are you?

GHOST
Am I really sentenced to remain in this
hateful place forever?

NIETZSCHE
Well I cannot think of any woman who
will sacrifice herself for your
redemption, can you?

The GHOST shakes his head.

CARD - FINALE.   THE REDEMPTION

NIETZSCHE
But there are three men who can save
you and every one of them is a Jew.

GHOST
Who? Not Meyerbeer?

NIETZSCHE
No not Meyerbeer. The first is Solti.

GHOST
Solti the conductor?

NIETZSCHE
Yes, this Jew wrote, 'I am not interested
in Wagner's political and philosophical
ideas, or his betrayal of friends. To me
anyone who can create such beauty,
whether he be half Jewish, anti-Semite,

76

liberal or royalist, is first and foremost a
musical genius and will remain so as
long as our civilization lasts.' So you see
Solti sacrificed his beliefs for your music.

The Ghost looks shamefaced.

NIETZSCHE
The second is Abraham Sabor.

GHOST
But Abraham Sabor is a Jewish
moneylender.

NIETZSCHE
Yes, to whom you owe a fortune, which
you have never made the slightest
attempt to pay back.

GHOST
How can he hold a key to my
redemption?

NIETZSCHE
Abraham Sabor told his son, 'I have just
given Wagner a lot of money. He hardly
said thank you. I told him I couldn't help
being a Jew, and he called me Shylock.
You see my son, the world is full of
people who borrow and don't repay;
who steal other men's wives, daughters
and sweethearts, many. But only one of
them wrote 'Tristram and Isolde'. I only

hope my child, when old age might make me bitter, you will not listen to me but will listen instead to the music of Wagner.'

Tristram and Isolde Music creeps in.

GHOST
Sabor said that?

NIETZSCHE
Yes. So you see Solti sacrificed his beliefs, and Abraham Sabor sacrificed his money for your music.

GHOST
Who is the last?

NIETZSCHE
Joseph Rubinstein.

GHOST
Joseph Rubinstein, Bayreuth's supreme young pianist? A brilliant soloist.

NIETZSCHE
One of many Jews you employed or worked with despite your self. The very year after you died, Joseph was so distraught at the loss that he committed suicide. Here is your final sacrificial lamb who gave his life for your music. On these three I add my own testimony.

GHOST

You? But you have just spent the night attacking my work.

NIETZSCHE

Your libretto. You always sent me your words a year, even two before I heard the music. As one of the few operatic composers who wrote his own libretto, the words were less than poetic, they seemed full of theoretical devises. But as you say you heard the music as you wrote the words. We could not hear them together till the finished piece. One can read the Mastersingers but you cannot hear the musical revolution till it is together. Everything that is you, your incomprehensible frustration at the way of the world are manifested in dramatic musical motives. Your ideologies forced your musical demands in to areas no other composer had ever been. Even Schopenhauer's theory of music being chords suspended in non conclusions created that most glorious moment in Tristram where each chord lifts and suspends, lifts and suspends on and on into a musical heaven of emotion. With my weakened eyes I could see anew - the blue music of Lohengrin, the rugged mountains of the Valkerie, the deep waters of 'Rhinegold' and the

79

atmospheric clear blue sky of those
suspended violins. Those who criticise,
like me, criticise the raw base complexity
of the man but those who have heard the
music are speechless. Are you still
there?

NIETZSCHE sits down exhausted. He puts on his glasses.

NIETZSCHE
Are you still there, Maestro?

GHOST
I am disappearing. I am disappearing.
Goodbye redeemer.

NIETZSCHE
Goodbye Maestro. No one will ever be
able to write music in the same way
again.

GHOST
And no one will be able to write
philosophy after you.

The GHOST disappears. NIETZSCHE is left alone,
motionless. The music of "Thus Sprach Zarathustra' seeps
slowly in. As the trumpets sound NIETZSCHE removes his
glasses and gets to his feet. The drum pounds as his
speech gets louder.

NIETZSCHE
The twilight of the Gods begins. What
follows will be the night of drums. When

the day returns there will be a world of
hope, a world where the natural will
dominate over the manufactured, where
ideas will dominate over prejudices, a
world of Supermen - wise, intelligent and
freethinking. The purpose of life is life, it
has no value or meaning apart from
itself. We will assert our presence
fighting to the very death for life. Spirits
of a new world will write music to that
rarefied creature, that giant of intellect
ZARATHUSTRA! ZARATHUSRA!
ZARATHUSTRA. ZARATHUSTRA

MATRON
Doctor! Orderlies! Help he's having
another fit!

BLACKOUT

FRIEDRICH NIETZSCHE never spoke another word and
spent the last ten years of his life in a permanents state of
catatonia.

CURTAIN

ABOUT THE AUTHOR

JULIAN Doyle is the editor of 'Life of Brian' and is also one of the world's most versatile filmmakers. He has written and directed his own films, and edited, photographed and created Fx on others. He is most famous for editing the Monty Python Films and shooting the Fxs for the Terry Gilliam films 'TimeBandits and 'Brazil', which he also edited.

He has written and directed three feature films. 'Love Potion' about a drug rehabilitation centre, described as Hitchcockian. 'Chemical Wedding' featuring Simon Callow about the outrageous British occultist, Aleister Crowley and described by one American reviewer as 'Thoroughly entertaining although at times you wonder if the film makers have not lost all there senses'. He has also directed award winning pop videos such as Kate Bush's 'Cloudbusting' featuring Donald Sutherland and Iron Maiden's 'Play with Madness'. This play 'Twilight of the Gods' was described by 'Philosophy Today' as 'Masterful!' Python's, Terry Jones has described him as an original Polymath.

Julian was born in London and started life in the slums of Paddington. His Irish father, Bob, was one of the youngest members of the International Brigade that went to fight against Franco's invasion of democratic Spain. His mother, Lola, was born in Spain of an Asturian miner who died early of silicosis. She was thereafter brought up in a Catholic orphanage in Oviedo.

Julian started his education at St. Saviours, a church primary school. He went on to Haverstock secondary school, one of the first comprehensive schools in England. His first job was as a junior technician to Professor Peter Medawar's team, which won the Nobel Prize soon after Julian's arrival. Not that he claims any credit for that. At night school he passed his 'A' level exams and took a Zoology degree at London University. After a year at the Institute of Education, he taught biology before going to the London Film School. On leaving he started a film company with other students. Besides film making, Julian is well known for his Masterclasses in Film Directing.

While still at school, Julian had a daughter, Margarita who was brought up in the family. He then had two further children, Jud and Jessie.

ALSO BY JULIAN DOYLE

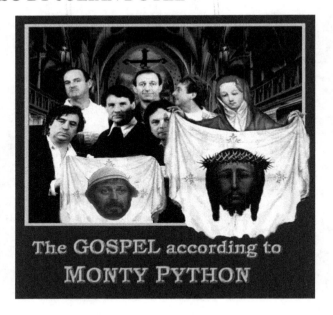

The GOSPEL according to
MONTY PYTHON

Who was the real Brian? Who was the real Jesus?
Who was the real Bishop of Southwark? Did the
Romans build the Jerusalem Aqueduct? Were the
Magi wise? And were the People's Front of Judea,
splitters? All the crucial questions this book attempts
to answer.

A wild, chaotic, bronco-busting ride in
An out-of-control fairground, but hang on
in there – it's worth it. *Terry Jones*

CPSIA information can be obtained
at www.ICGtesting.com
Printed in the USA
LVHW081519031020
667858LV00007B/337